ACT III
SCENE I
SCENE II
SCENE III
SCENE IV
SCENE V
SCENE VI
SCENE VII
SCENE VIII
SCENE IX
SCENE X
ACT IV
SCENE I
SCENE II
SCENE III
SCENE IV
SCENE V
SCENE VI
SCENE VII
SCENE VIII
SCENE IX
SCENE X
ACT V
SCENE I
SCENE II
SCENE III
SCENE IV
SCENE V
SCENE VI
SCENE VII
MARGARET CAVENDISH - A CONCISE BIBLIOGRAPHY

THE NAMES OF THE PERSONS

Monsieur Generosity
Monsieur Nobilissimo
Monsieur Perfection
Monsieur Importunate
Monsieur Bon Compaignon
Monsieur Profession
Monsieur Comorade
Monsieur Discretion
Monsieur Compliment.
Doctor Freedom, a Doctor of Physick
Madam La Mere
Madamosel Caprisia
Madamosel Doltche

Madamosel Solid
Madamosel Volante
A Grave Matron
Madamosel Doltches
Nurse
Two Maid-servants

PROLOGUE

This Play I do present to Lady wits,
And hope the wit, each several humour fits;
For though all wit, be wit, as of wit kind,
Yet different be, as men, not of one mind;
For different men, hath different minds we know,
So different Wits, in different humours flow.
The cholerick Wit is rough, and salt as brine,
The humble Wit flows smooth, in a strait line:
A wise Wit flows in streams, fresh, pure and clear,
Where neither weeds, nor troubled waves appear:
But a wild wit in every ditch doth flow,
And with the mudde doth soul, and filthy grow.

ACT I

SCENE I

Enter **MADAMOSEL CAPRISIA**, and her **MAID**

MAID
Madam, Monsieur Importunate is come to visit you.

MADAMOSEL CAPRISIA
Did not I tell you, I would receive no visits to day.

MAID
I did tell him that you desired to be excused; but he said, he would not excuse you, for he must see you.

MADAMOSEL CAPRISIA
Go tell him I have taken Physick.

MAID
I did tell him so, but he said, he would stay untill it had done working.

The Comedy Named the Several Wits by Margaret Cavendish

Margaret Lucas Cavendish, Duchess of Newcastle-upon-Tyne was born in 1623 in Colchester, Essex into a family of comfortable means.

As the youngest of eight children she spent much time with her siblings. Margaret had no formal education but she did have access to scholarly libraries and tutors, although she later said the children paid little attention to the tutors, who were there 'rather for formality than benefit'.

From an early age Margaret was already assembling her thoughts for future works despite the then conditions of society that women did not partake in public authorship. For England it was also a time of Civil War. The Royalists were being pushed back and Parliamentary forces were in the ascendancy.

Despite these obvious dangers, when Queen Henrietta Maria was in Oxford, Margaret asked her mother for permission to become one of her Ladies-in-waiting. She was accepted and, in 1644, accompanied the Queen into exile in France. This took her away from her family for the first time.

Despite living at the Court of the young King Louis XIV, life for the young Margaret was not what she expected. She was far from her home and her confidence had been replaced by shyness and difficulties fitting in to the grandeur of her surroundings and the eminence of her company.

Margaret told her mother she wanted to leave the Court. Her mother was adamant that she should stay and not disgrace herself by leaving. She provided additional funds for her to make life easier. Margaret remained. It was now also that she met and married William Cavendish who, at the time, was the Marquis of Newcastle (and later Duke). He was also 30 years her senior and previously married with two children.

As Royalists, a return to life in England was not yet possible. They would remain in exile in Paris, Rotterdam and Antwerp until the restoration of the crown in 1660 although Margaret was able to return for attention to some estate matters.

Along with her husband's brother, Sir Charles Cavendish, she travelled to England after having been told that her husband's estate (taken from him due to his being a royalist) was to be sold and that she, as his wife, would receive some benefit of the sale. She received nothing. She left England to be with her husband again.

The couple were devoted to each other. Margaret wrote that he was the only man she was ever in love with, loving him not for title, wealth or power, but for merit, justice, gratitude, duty, and fidelity. She also relied upon him for support in her career. The marriage provided no children despite efforts made by her physician to overcome her inability to conceive.

Margaret's first book, 'Poems and Fancies', was published in 1653; it was a collection of poems, epistles and prose pieces which explores her philosophical, scientific and aesthetic ideas.

For a woman at this time writing and publishing were avenues they had great difficulty in pursuing. Added to this was Margaret's range of subjects. She wrote across a number of issues including gender, power, manners, scientific method, and philosophy.

She always claimed she had too much time on her hands and was therefore able to indulge her love of writing. As a playwright she produced many works although most are as closet dramas. (This is a play not intended to be performed onstage, but instead read by a solitary reader or perhaps out loud in a small group. For Margaret the rigours of exile, her gender and Cromwell's closing of the theatres mean this was her early vehicle of choice and, despite these handicaps, she became one of the most well-known playwrights in England)

Her utopian romance, 'The Blazing World', (1666) is one of the earliest examples of science fiction. Margaret also published extensively in natural philosophy and early modern science; at least a dozen books.

She was the first woman to attend a meeting at Royal Society of London in 1667 and she criticized and engaged with members and philosophers Thomas Hobbes, René Descartes, and Robert Boyle.

Margaret was always defended against any criticism by her husband and he also contributed to some of her works. She also gives him credit as her writing tutor.

Perhaps a little strangely she said her ambition despite her shyness, was to have everlasting fame. During her career, from the mid 1650's until her death, she was prolific. In recent decades her work has undergone a resurgence of interest propelled mainly by her ground-breaking attitude and accomplishments in those male straitened times.

Margaret Cavendish died on 15th December 1673 and was buried at Westminster Abbey.

Index of Contents
THE NAMES OF THE PERSONS
THE COMEDY NAMED THE SEVERAL WITS
PROLOGUE
ACT I
SCENE I
SCENE II
SCENE III
SCENE IV
SCENE V
SCENE VI
SCENE VII
ACT II
SCENE I
SCENE II
SCENE III
SCENE IV
SCENE V
SCENE VI
SCENE VII
SCENE VIII
SCENE IX

MADAMOSEL CAPRISIA
I would it were working in his belly.

[Exit.

SCENE II

Enter **MADAMOSEL VOLANTE**, and **MONSIEUR BON CAMPAIGNON**.

MONSIEUR BON CAMPAIGNON
Lady, hearing of your great wit, I am come to prove report.

MADAMOSEL VOLANTE
You will find him a lyer, Sir.

MONSIEUR BON CAMPAIGNON
I had rather report should be a lyer, than I a Lover.

MADAMOSEL VOLANTE
Why, then we agree in a mind, for I had rather be thought a fool, than to be troubled with a fools company.

MONSIEUR BON CAMPAIGNON
You need not be troubled with that, for love is strongest absented.

MADAMOSEL VOLANTE
O! but there is an old Proverb, that love will break thorough stone-walls, wherefore if you be in love, you will haunt me like a Fairy, no locks nor bolts will keep you out, for fairy love will creep thorough a creavice.

MONSIEUR BON CAMPAIGNON
Faith Lady! I find now, that love is the Queen of Fayries, for it hath crept thorough the key-hole of my eares, and hath got into my head, and their dances such roundelayes, as makes my brain dissie.

MADAMOSEL VOLANTE
If once your brain begins to be dissie, your senses will stagger, and your reason will fall down from its feat, and when the reason is displaced, and the wit is distemper'd, the mind become mad, and to prevent the mischief that may follow, I will depart in time.

[Exit.

SCENE III

Enter **MADAMOSEL CAPRISIA**, as at the door meets **MONSIEUR IMPORTUNATE**, he stops her passage.

MONSIEUR IMPORTUNATE
You shall not pass, untill you have paid me a tribute.

MADAMOSEL CAPRISIA
What Tribute?

MONSIEUR IMPORTUNATE
A kiss.

MADAMOSEL CAPRISIA
I will pay no such tribute, for I will bring such a number of words armed with such strong reasons, as they shall make my way.

MONSIEUR IMPORTUNATE
Your words will prove poor Pilgrims, which come to offer at the Altar of my lips.

MADAMOSEL CAPRISIA
Nay, rather than so, they shall come as humble Petitioners, and as it were, kneeling at your heart, shall with innocency beg for gentle civility.

MONSIEUR IMPORTUNATE
I will shut the gates of my ears against them, and my lips as a bar shall force them back, being a precise factious rout.

MADAMOSEL CAPRISIA
Satire shall lead my sharp words on, break ope those gates, and anger like consuming fire shall both destroy your will and base desire.

MONSIEUR IMPORTUNATE
I will try that.

MADAMOSEL CAPRISIA
But I will rather make a safe retreat, than venture, least your rude strength might overcome my words.

[She goeth back, he follows her

MONSIEUR IMPORTUNATE
I will march after, at the heels of you.

[Exit.

SCENE IV

Enter **MADAMOSEL DOLTCHE**, and **MONSIEUR COMPLIMENT**.

MADAMOSEL DOLTCHE

Sir, you prayse me so much, as I may doubt, or rather believe you flatter me; for it is not possible to be so rare a creature, as you express me to be, unless I were something divine, perchance I may be worthy of some of your inferiour Prayses, but not all your high and mighty ones.

MONSIEUR COMPLIMENT

You are more than either I can express, or think you to be.

MADAMOSEL DOLTCHE

Nay, if I be above your thoughts, I am above your delight; for man-kind takes no great pleasure in that they comprehend not.

MONSIEUR COMPLIMENT

I believe you do not comprehend how well I love you.

MADAMOSEL DOLTCHE

No truely, for love is like infinite, it hath no circumference, wherefore I will not trouble my self in loves wayes, since it is an endlesse journey.

MONSIEUR COMPLIMENT

But surely, Lady, though you cannot find that worth in me, as merits your esteem and affection, yet you will favour me for your lathers command, and love me for his desire.

MADAMOSEL DOLTCHE

If my Father desires me to dye, I shall satisfie his desire, for it is in my power to take away my own life, when I will; but it is not in my power to love those my Father would have me; for love is not to be commanded, nor directed, nor governed, nor prescribed, for love is free, and not to be controuled; Also I may marry a man my Father desires me, but sure my Father will not desire, nor command me to marry, if I cannot love the man he would have me marry, as I ought to do a Husband.

[Exit.

SCENE V

Enter **MADAMOSEL CAPRISIA**, and a Grave **MATRON**.

MATRON

Madamosel Caprisia, there is a Gentleman, one of my acquaintance doth desire to see you.

MADAMOSEL CAPRISIA

He desires more than I do, for I never see a man, but I wish a vail before my sight, or one before his.

MATRON

Have you taken a surfeit of eyes, as you hate to look on a mans face.

MADAMOSEL CAPRISIA
Yes, of wanton eyes, that skips from face to face, which makes me love the blind.

MATRON
I wonder whether the soul may be satisfied, or surfeit as the senses do.

MADAMOSEL CAPRISIA
The thoughts, passions and appetites, which are begot betwixt the soul and senses, will surfeit, if they be over-fed.

[Enter **MONSIEUR BON CAMPAIGNON**.

MONSIEUR BON CAMPAIGNON
What is that Lady that is over-fed?

MADAMOSEL CAPRISIA
A fools-head.

MONSIEUR BON CAMPAIGNON
How can a fools head be over-fed?

MADAMOSEL CAPRISIA
With hearing and seeing more than it can digest into understanding.

MONSIEUR BON CAMPAIGNON
You have not such a head, Lady, for your head is so full of wit, as it perpetually flows thorough your lips; yet whatsoever it doth receive, the Son of reason doth digest, and refines into spirits of senses.

MADAMOSEL CAPRISIA
I must confess, my tongue is more fertil than my brain, the which comes more words from the one, than sense or reason from the other; but least I should over-fill your ears with my idle talks, I will leave you.

[Exit.

MONSIEUR BON CAMPAIGNON
And I will follow you, for my ears are unsatisfied, having but a taste of her wit, which makes a greater appetite.

[**MONSIEUR BON CAMPAIGNON**, and **MATRON** Exit.

SCENE VI

Enter **MADAMOSEL SOLID, MONSIEUR PROFESSION,** and **MONSIEUR COMORADE** his friend.

MONSIEUR PROFESSION
Lady, you live, as if you lived not, living so solitary a life.

MADAMOSEL SOLID

Indeed, few doth live as they should, that is, to live within themselves; for the soul, which is the supream part of the life, is never at home, but goeth wandering about, from place to place, from person to person, and so from one thing to another, and not only the soul wanders thus; but all the Family of the soul, as the thoughts and passions; for should any thing knock at the gates of the soul, which are the senses, or enter the chambers of the soul, which is the heart, and the head, they would find them empty, for the thoughts and passions, which passions are of the Bed-chamber, which is, the heart and Presence-chamber, which is, the head wherein they ought to wait, are for the most part, all gone abroad; as for the thoughts, they are gone to inquire news, walking and running into every Village, Town, City and Country, and Kingdom, all to inquire what such and such persons said or acted, and the particular affairs of every particular person, and every particular Family, as whether they increase with riches, or decay with poverty; whether they live beyond their means, or keep within their compasse; what men and women are in love, who are constant, and who are false; what contracts are signed, or what contracts are broken; who marries, and who lives single lives; who is happy in marriage, and who is not; what children is born, who hath children, and who hath none; who is handsome, and who is ill-favoured; who dyes, and of what diseases they died of; whether they left wealth or were poor, or who were their Heirs, or Executors; who are Widowers, Widows or Orphants; who hath losses, crosses and misfortunes, who is in favour or disgrace with such Princes or States; who is at Law, what suits there is lost or gained; what bribes were given and taken, who was arrested, or imprisoned for debts; or set in the Pillary or Stocks for disorder, or cast into the Counter for misdemeanour; who is accused or imprisoned for Robbery, Murther or Treason; who is condemned or reprieved; what deaths they died, or torments indur'd; what Laws there is made, repeald or broke; what Officers or Magistrates there are made, plac'd or displac'd, or put out; what factions or bruleries there is, what leagues and associates there is made betwixt States and Princes; What Wars, or Peace there is, or like to be betwixt such or such Kingdoms; What triumphs, or shews there is, or like to be; What Mountebanks, Tumblers, and Dancers there is; What strange Birds, Beasts or Monsters there is to be seen; what Drunkards, Bawds and Whores there is, What Debts hath been sought, and the cause of their quarrels; who hath lost at play, and Who hath Won, What new fashions there is; What Stuffs, Silks, Laces, and Imbroideries there is; What Lords, Ladyes, Knights or Esquires hath new Coaches or Liveries; What rich cloths they had, or have; what Church is most frequented, What Balls, Masks, Plays & Feasts there is, or like to be, and many the like vain, idle, unusefull, unprofitable inquiries, observations and entertainments; their thoughts imployes and Wasts their time With: as for the passions and affections, they are as much abroad, as the rest of the thoughts, some being With such and such men, or such and such Women, as first with one, and then with another; or with such a house, or houses, or lands, or with such Jewels, or Place, or Hangings, or Pictures, or the like; also the passions and affections wander; amongst Beasts, as with such a Horse, Dog, Monkey, or the like; or with Birds, as with such a Hawk, Cock of the Game, or prating Parrot, or singing Linet, or the like; or the passions and affections are attending, watching, or seeking after such or such Offices or Commands, Governments or Titles; nay, the very soul itself goeth after such and such designes, so as it doth, as it were, run away from it self, it follows the World, and worldly things, but never draws any benefit to it self, but that soul that keeps at home, which very few souls doth; imployes it self, for it self, it only views the World for knowledge, yet so, as it looks, as out of a window on a prospect, it uses the World out of necessity, but not serves the World out of slavery; it is industrious for its own tranquility, fame and everlasting life, for which it leaves nothing unsought, or undone, is a wise soul.

MONSIEUR PROFESSION

Madam, my soul is tyed to your soul, with such an undissoulable knot of affection, that nothing, no, not death can lose it, nor break it asunder; wherefore, wheresoever your soul doth go, thine will follow it, and bear it company.

MADAMOSEL SOLID
Then your soul Will be incognita, for my soul Will not know whether your soul will be with it, or not.

[Exit.

MONSIEUR COMORADE
Faith Thom. its happy for thy soul, to be drawn by her magnetick soul; for that may draw, lead or direct thy soul to Heaven; otherwise thy soul will fall into Hell with the pressure of they sins, for thy soul is as heavy, as crime can make it.

MONSIEUR PROFESSION
Why, then the divel would have found my soul an honest soul, in being full weight, his true coyn, & the right stamp of his Picture, or Figure, for Which he would have used my soul well, and if Heaven gives me not this, Lady, Hell take me.

MONSIEUR COMORADE
Certainly you may be the Divels guest, but whether you will be the Ladys Husband, it is to be doubted.

MONSIEUR PROFESSION
Well, I will do my endeavour to get her, and more, a man cannot do.

[Exit.

[Enter **MADAMOSEL CAPRISIA**, and **MONSIEUR IMPORTUNATE**.

MONSIEUR IMPORTUNATE
You are the rarest beauty, and greatest wit in the World.

MADAMOSEL CAPRISIA
Wit is like beauty, and beauty is oftener created in the fancie, than the face; so wit oftener by opinion, than in the brain, not, but surely there may be a real beauty, and so a real wit, yet that real wit, is no wit to the ignorant, no more than beauty to the blind, for the wit is lost to the understanding, as beauty is lost to the eyes, and it is not in nature to give, what is not in nature to receive, nor in nature to shew what is not in nature to be seen; so there must be eyes to see beauty, and eares to hear wit, and understanding to judge of both, and you have neither judgments eyes, nor understandings ears, nor rational sense.

MONSIEUR IMPORTUNATE
Why, then you have neither beauty nor wit.

MADAMOSEL CAPRISIA
I have both, but your commendations are from report; for fools speaks by rote, as Parrots do.

[Exit. Monsieur Importunate solus.

MONSIEUR IMPORTUNATE
She is like a Bee loaded with sweet honey, but her tongue is the sting, that blisters all it strikes on.

[Exit.

Enter **MADAMOSEL VOLANTE**, and **MONSIEUR BON COMPAIGNON**.

MONSIEUR BON CAMPAIGNON
Lady, why are you so silent.

MADAMOSEL VOLANTE
Why soul I speak to those that understands me not.

MONSIEUR BON CAMPAIGNON
Why? are you so difficult to be understood.

MADAMOSEL VOLANTE
No, but understanding is so difficult to find.

MONSIEUR BON CAMPAIGNON
So, and since there is such a total decay of understanding in every brain, as there is none to be found, but in your own, you will make a new Common-wealth in yours, where your thoughts, as wife Magistrates, and good Citizens, shall govern and traffick therein, and your words shall be as Letters of Mart, and your senses shall be as legate Embassadors that lives in other Kingdoms, which takes instructions, and give intelligence, or rather your thoughts are destinies, and fates, and your words their several decrees.

MADAMOSEL VOLANTE
Do you think my thoughts can warrant Laws, or can my words decree them?

MONSIEUR BON CAMPAIGNON
I believe your thoughts are so wise and just, that whatsoever they allow of, must be best, and your words are so witty, rational; positive and powerfull, as none can contradict them.

MADAMOSEL VOLANTE
Good Sir, contradict your self, or Truth will contradict you.

MONSIEUR BON CAMPAIGNON
Nay faith, I will never take the pains to contradict my self; let Truth do what she will.

[Exit.

Enter **MADAM LA MERE**, and her daughter **MADAMOSEL CAPRISIA**.

MADAM LA MERE
Daughter, did you entertain the Lady Visit civilly?

MADAMOSEL CAPRISIA
Yes Mother, extraordinary civilly, for I gave her leave to entertain herself with her own discourse.

MADAM LA MERE
That was rudely.

MADAMOSEL CAPRISIA
O no, for certainly it is the height of courtship to our sex, to let them talk all the talk themselves; for all women takes more delight to discourse themselves, than to hear another; and they are extreamly pleased, if any listens, or at lest seems to listen to them, For the truth is, that talking is one of the most luxurious appetites women have; wherefore I could not be more civiller, than to bar and restrain the effeminate nature in my self, to give her tongue liberty.

MADAM LA MERE
But you should have spoken a word now, and then, as giving her civilly some breathing rest for her discourse to lean upon.

MADAMOSEL CAPRISIA
Her speech was so strong, and long-winded, as it run with a full speed, without stop or stay, it neither need spurre nor whip; the truth is it had been well, if it had been held in with the bridle of moderation, for it ran quite beyond the bounds of discretion, although sometimes it ran upon the uneven wayes of slander, other times upon the stony ground of censure, and sometimes in the soul wayes of immodesty, and often upon the furrows of non-sense; besides, it did usually skip over the hedges of Truth, and certainly, if the necessities of nature, and the separations of Neigh-bourhood, and the changes and inter-course of, and in the affairs of the World, and men did not forcibly stop, sometimes a womans tongue, it would run as far as the confines of death.

MADAM LA MERE
But let me tell you Daughter, your tongue is as sharp, as a Serpents sting, and will wound as cruelly and deadly where it bites.

MADAMOSEL CAPRISIA
It proves my tongue a womans tongue.

MADAM LA MERE
Why should a womans tongue have the effects of a Serpents sting.

MADAMOSEL CAPRISIA

The reason is evident, for the great Serpent that tempted, and so perverted our Grandmother Eve in Paradise, had a monstrous sting, and our Grandmother whetted her tongue with his sting, and ever since, all her effeminate rase hath tongues that stings.

[Exit.

SCENE II

Enter **MADAMOSEL DOLTCHE**, and **MONSIEUR BON CAMPAIGNON**.

MONSIEUR BON CAMPAIGNON
Lady, Monsieur Nobilissimo is so in love with you, as he cannot be happy, untill you be his wife.

MADAMOSEL DOLTCHE
I wonder he should be in love with me, since I have neither beauty to allure him, nor so much riches, as to intice him, nor wit to perswade him to marry me.

MONSIEUR BON CAMPAIGNON
But Lady, you have vertue, good nature, sweet disposition, gracefull behaviour, which are sufficient Subjects for love to settle on, did you want what you mentioned, out you have all, not only what any man can with or desire with a wife, but you have as much as you can wish and desire to have your self.

MADAMOSEL DOLTCHE
I will rather be so vain, as to strive to believe you, than rudely to contradict you.

MONSIEUR BON CAMPAIGNON
It is neither erroneous, nor vain to believe a truth, Lady.

MADAMOSEL DOLTCHE
Nor civil to make a doubt, Sir; but I am obliged unto you for that, you help to cover my defects, and wants in nature, with your civil commendation, and your kind estimation of me.

[Exit.

SCENE III

Enter **MONSIEUR IMPORTUNATE**, and **MADAMOSEL CAPRISIA**.

MONSIEUR IMPORTUNATE
My fair wit, you look as if you were angry with me.

MADAMOSEL CAPRISIA
You dwell not so long in my mind, as to make me angry, my thoughts are strangers to your figures.

[She offers to go away, and he holds her from going.

MONSIEUR IMPORTUNATE
Nay faith, now I have you, I will keep you perforce, untill you pay me the kiss you owe me.

MADAMOSEL CAPRISIA
Let me go, for I had rather my eyes were eternally seal'd up, my ears for ever stopt close from sound, than hear or see you.

MONSIEUR IMPORTUNATE
I care not whether you hear, or see me, so you will kisse me.

MADAMOSEL CAPRISIA
Let me go, or otherwise my lips shall curse you, and my words being whetted with injurie, are become so sharp, as they will wound you.

MONSIEUR IMPORTUNATE
I will keep you untill your words begs for mercy in the most humblest stile, and after the most mollifying manner.

MADAMOSEL CAPRISIA
Hell take you, or Earth devoure you like a beast, never to rise.

MONSIEUR IMPORTUNATE
Love strike your heart with shooting thorough your eyes.

MADAMOSEL CAPRISIA
May you be blown up with pride, untill you burst into madnesse, may your thoughts be more troubled than rough waters, more raging than a tempest; may your senses feel no pleasure, your body find no rest, nor your life any peace.

MONSIEUR IMPORTUNATE
May you love me with a doting affection; may I be the only man you will imbrace, and may you think me to be as handsome as Narcissus did himself.

MADAMOSEL CAPRISIA
You appear to me in all the horrid shapes that fancy can invent.

[Enter **MADAM LA MERE**.

MADAM LA MERE
Why, how now daughter, alwayes quarreling.

MADAMOSEL CAPRISIA
Can you blame me, when I am beset with rudeness, and assaulted with uncivil actions.

MADAM LA MERE
Let her alone, Monsieur Importunate, for she is a very Shrew.

MONSIEUR IMPORTUNATE
Well, go thy wayes, for all the Shrews that ever nature made, you are the cursest one.

[Exit.

Enter **MADAMOSEL VOLANTE**, and a Grave **MATRON**.

MADAMOSEL VOLANTE
I am not of the humour; as most Women are, Which is, to please themselves With thinking, or rather believing, that all men that looks on them, are in love With them: But I take pleasure, that all men that I look on, should think I am in love With them; Which men Will soon believe, being as self-conceited as Women are.

MATRON
But Where is the pleasure, Lady.

MADAMOSEL VOLANTE
Why, in seeing their phantastical garbs, their strutting postures, their smiling faces, and the jackanapesly actions, and then I laugh in my mind, to think what fools they are, so as I make my self merry at their folly, and not at my own.

MATRON
But men will appear as much Jackanapeses, when they are in love with you, as if they thought you were in love with them, for all Lovers are apish, more or less.

MADAMOSEL VOLANTE
I grant all Lovers are, but those that think themselves beloved, appears more like the grave Babboon, than the skipping Iackanapes; for though their actions are as ridiculous, yet they are with more formality, as being more circumspectly foolish, or self-conceitedly vain.

MATRON
Well, for all your derisions and gesting at men, I shall see you at onetime or other, shot with Cupids arrow.

MADAMOSEL VOLANTE
By deaths dart, you may; but never by loves arrow; for death hath power on me, though love hath none.

MATRON
There is an old saying, that time, importunity and opportunity, wins the chastest She, when those are joyned with wealth and dignity; but to yield to a lawfull love, neither requires much time, nor pleading, if the Suiters have but Person, Title and wealth, which women for the most part do prize, before valour, wisdom or honesty.

MADAMOSEL VOLANTE
Women hath reason to prefer certainties before uncertainties; for mens Persons, Titles and Wealths, are visible to their view and knowledge, but their Valours, Wisdoms and Honesties, doth rest upon Faith; for a coward may fight, and a fool may speak rationally, and act prudently sometimes, and a knave may appear an honest man.

MATRONS
They may so, but a valiant man, will never act the part of a coward; nor a wise man prove a fool, nor an honest man appear a knave.

MADAMOSEL VOLANTE
There can be no proof of any mans Valour, Wisdom or Honesty, but at the day of his death, in aged years, when as he hath past the danger in Wars, the tryals in Miseries, the malice of Fortune, the temptations of Pleasures, the inticements of Vice, the heights of Glory, the changes of Life, provokers of Passion, deluders of Senses, torments of Pain, or painfull Torments, and to chose a Husband that hath had the Tryals, and experiences of all these, is to chose a Husband out of the Grave, and rather than I will marry death, I will live a maid, as long as I live, and when I dye, let death do what he will with me.

[Exit.

SCENE V

Enter **MONSIEUR PROFESSION** in mourning; then enters his Friend, **MONSIEUR COMORADE**.

MONSIEUR COMORADE
Well met, I have travelled thorough all the Town, and have inquired of every one I could speak to, and could neither hear of thee, nor see thee.

MONSIEUR PROFESSION
It were happy for me, if I had neither ears nor eyes.

MONSIEUR COMORADE
Why, what is the matter, man?

[He observes his mourning and then starts.

Gods-me! Now I perceive thou art in mourning: which of thy Friends is dead?

MONSIEUR PROFESSION
The chiefest friend I had, which mas my heart; For that is dead, being kill'd with my Mistress cruelty, and buryed in her inconstancy.

MONSIEUR COMORADE
I dare swear, not the whole heart; for every mans heart, is like a head of Garlick, which may be divided into many several cloves: Wherefore, cheer up, man; for it is but one clove, that death, or love, hath swallowed down into his Stomach, to cure him of the wind-cholick; and since thy heart hath so many

cloves, thou mayst well spare him one, and be never the worse; But if it be buryed, as you say, in your Mistresses inconstancy; it is to be hop'd it will be converted into the same inconstant humour, and that will cure the other part of thy heart.

MONSIEUR PROFESSION
O! She was the Saint of my thoughts, and the Goddesse of my soul.

MONSIEUR COMORADE
Prethee let me be thy moral Tutor, to instruct thee in the knowledge of Truth, and to let thee know, that vertue is the true Goddesse, to which all men ought to bow to; and that youth, beauty and wealth, are sixt to be forsaken, when vertue comes in place; and vertue is constant, both to its principals and promises; Wherefore, if thy Mistresse be inconstant, she cannot be vertuous, wherefore let her go.

[**MONSIEUR PROFESSION** setches a great sigh, and goes out without speaking a word. Comorade alone.

MONSIEUR COMORADE
I think his heart is dead in good earnest; for it hath no sense of what I have said.

[Exit.

SCENE VI

Enter **MADAM LA MERE**, and her Daughter **MADAMOSEL CAPRISIA**.

MADAM LA MERE
Daughter, you have a sufficiency of wit and beauty, to get many Lovers to chose a Husband, if you had but patience to entertain, and prudence to keep them; But your being crosse, will lose your Lovers, as soon as your beauty hath taken them.

MADAMOSEL CAPRISIA
It is no prize for a woman to have such Lovers, that hath amorous natures; for it is their nature that drives them to her, and not the womans beauty or wit, that draws them to her; and there is less force required to drive, than to draw; but the truth is, that most men hath such threed-bare souls, as if the nap of their understanding were worn of; or indeed, their souls seems, as if there were never any woven thereon, as that nature hath made all their souls, thin and course, or as if time had Moath-eaten them, which makes me, although not to hate you, yet to despise that Sex; for men that should imitate the Gods, yet are they worse than Beasts, which makes me shun their beastly company.

MADAM LA MERE
Daughter, you speak and judge passionately, and passion can never reason well; for how is it possible, for reason to exercise its function, when passion opposes, and is too strong for it.

MADAMOSEL CAPRISIA
Truth may be delivered in passion, but not corrupted with passion; for truth is truth, howsoever it be divulged, or else it is no truth, but falsehood.

[Exit.

Enter **MONSIEUR PERFECTION**, and **MADAMOSEL SOLID**, drest very fine.

MONSIEUR PERFECTION
You are wondrous fine, to day, Madam.

MADAMOSEL SOLID
If I seem fine, to day, I am obliged more to my fancie, than my wealth, for this finerie.

MONSIEUR PERFECTION
The truth is, you are so adjousted, so curiously accoutred, as I perceive, judgement and wit were joyned associates in your dressing.

MADAMOSEL SOLID
I had rather be commended, or applauded for judgement and wit, than for wealth and beauty; for I had rather have my soul commended, than my person, or fortunes.

MONSIEUR PERFECTION
Certainly, I believe you have a more rational soul, than any other of your Sex have.

MADAMOSEL SOLID
Alas? My soul is but a young soul, a meer Novice soul, it wants growth, or my soul is like a house, which time the architectour hath newly begun to build; and the senses, which are the Labourers, wants information and experience, which are the materiall for the rational soul to be built on, or with; but such materials as hath been brought in, I strive and endeavour to make the best, and most convenient use for a happy life.

MONSIEUR PERFECTION
How say you? the best use for a good Wife!

MADAMOSEL SOLID
No, that little reason I have, tells me, to be a Wife, is to be unhappy, for content seldom in marriage dwells, disturbance keeps possession.

MONSIEUR PERFECTION
If you disprayse marriage, you will destroy my hopes, and frustrate my honest design.

MADAMOSEL SOLID
Why? what is your design?

MONSIEUR PERFECTION
To be a Suiter to you.

MADAMOSEL SOLID
And what is your hopes?

MONSIEUR PERFECTION
To be your Husband.

MADAMOSEL SOLID
If I thought marriage were necessary, although unhappy, yet there would be required more wit and judgement in chosing a Husband than in dressing my self; wherefore it were requisite, that some of more wit and judgement than my self, should chose for me, otherwise I may be betray'd by flattery, outward garb, insinuations or false-hood, and through an unexperienced innocency, I may take words and shews, for worth and merit, which I pray the Gods I may not do; for to marry an unworthy man, were to me to be at the height of affliction, and marriage being unhappy in it self, needs no addition to make it worse.

MONSIEUR PERFECTION
Madam? Discretion forbids me to commend my self, although I am a Lover; For had I merits worthy great praises, it were unfit I should mention them; but there is not any man or woman, that is, or can be exactly known, either by themselves or others; for nature is obscure, she never divulges herself, neither to any creature, nor by, or through any creature; for the hides herself under infinite varieties, changes and chances; She disguises herself with antick Vizards, she appears sometimes old, sometimes young, sometimes vaded and withered, sometimes green and flourishing, sometimes feeble and weak, sometimes strong and lusty, sometimes deformed, and sometimes beautifull; sometimes she appears with horrour, sometimes with delight, sometimes she appears in glimsing lights of knowledge, then clouds herself with ignorance. But, Madam, since we are as ignorant of our souls, as of our fortunes, and as ignorant of our lives, as of our deaths; we cannot make any choice upon certainties, but upon uncertainties, and if we be good whilst we live, our deaths will be our witnesse to prove it; in the mean time, let our promises stand bound for us, which is the best ingagement we can give; although it may sail; and let our marriage be as the Bond of agreement, although we may forfeit the same, yet let us make it as sure as we can.

MADAMOSEL SOLID
I will consider it, and then I will answer your request.

MONSIEUR PERFECTION
That is, to yield.

MADAMOSEL SOLID
It is like enough.

[Exit.

SCENE VIII

Enter **MADAMOSEL CAPRISIA**, and **MONSIEUR IMPORTUNATE**.

MONSIEUR IMPORTUNATE
My fair Shrew, are you walking alone.

MADAMOSEL CAPRISIA
My thoughts are my best Companions.

MONSIEUR IMPORTUNATE
Pray, let a thought of me be one of the company.

MADAMOSEL CAPRISIA
When you enter into my mind, you do appear so mean, as my nobler thoughts, scorns that thought that bears your figure.

MONSIEUR IMPORTUNATE
Thoughts are as notes, and the tongue is the Fiddle that makes the musick; but your words, as the cords, are out of tune.

MADAMOSEL CAPRISIA
You say so, by reason they are not set to your humour, to sound your prayse.

MONSIEUR IMPORTUNATE
I say you are very handsome, nature hath given you a surpassing beauty, but pride and self-conceit, hath cast such a shadow, as it hath darkened it, as vaporous clowds doth the bright Sun.

MADAMOSEL CAPRISIA
Your opinions are clowdy, and your tongue like thunder, strikes my ears with rude, uncivil words.

[Exit. He alone.

MONSIEUR IMPORTUNATE
I perceive humility, dwels not with beauty, nor with; but is, as great a stranger, as with Riches and Titles.

[Exit.

SCENE IX

Enter **MADAMOSEL VOLANTE**, and **MONSIEUR DISCRETION**.

MONSIEUR DISCRETION
Madam, the same of your wit, drew me hither.

MADAMOSEL VOLANTE
I am sorry my wit hath a greater fame, than my worth, that my vain words should spread further than my vertuous actions, for noble fame is built on worthy deeds.

MONSIEUR DISCRETION

But it were pity you should bury your wit in silence; Besides, your discourse may profit the hearers, either with delight or instructions.

MADAMOSEL VOLANTE
O no, for discourses pleases according to the humour, or understanding of the hearers; Besides, it is the nature of mankind, to think each other fools, and none but themselves wise; Then why should I wast my life to no purpose, knowing times motion swift.

MONSIEUR DISCRETION
You do not wast your life through your words, if your words gets you a fame, and esteem of the World.

MADAMOSEL VOLANTE
What shall I be the better, in having the Worlds esteem, nay, it is likely that prayses (whilst I live) may do me harm, creating vain and false opinions in my imaginations of self-conceit, of being wiser, or wittier, than really I am; which opinions may make me commit errors, and I had rather the World should laugh at me, for want of wit, than scorn me for my follies.

MONSIEUR DISCRETION
But if witty discourses, will get you an esteem, what will your wise actions, and vertuous life; and prayse is the reward to all noble endeavours; beside, prayse is no burthen, but it often serves as a ballance, to make the life swim steady in Sea-faring World: But yet, Lady, I would not have your wit out-run your prayse, which it will do, if you spur it too hard, for wit must be used like a strong spirited horse, it must be restraind with a bridle, not prick'd with the spur, least it should run away, and fling the Rider, which is, the Speaker, into a ditch of disgrace; neither must it run wildly about, but must be wrought, to obey the hand and the heel, which is, time and occasion, to stop, and to change, as when to speak, and to whom to speak, and on what to speak, and when to make a stop of silence, otherwise, it will run out of the smooth paths of civility, or the clean wayes of modesty: Besides, wit must not only be taught, to amble in rhime, and to trot in prose, but to have a sure footing of sense, and a setled head of reason, least it should stumble in disputes, or fall into impertinent discourses; likewise, wit may be taught to go in aires of fancies, or low, upon the ground of proof.

MADAMOSEL VOLANTE
But Sir, you must consider, that women are no good managers of wit, for they spoyl all their tongue rides on, hackneys it out, untill it becomes a dull jade.

MONSIEUR DISCRETION
Least I should give an ill example of tyreing in our allegorical discourse, I shall kiss your hands, and take my leave for this time.

[Exit. **MADAMOSEL VOLANTE**. She fetches a great sigh.

MADAMOSEL VOLANTE
Monsieur Discretion is a handsom man, he hath a wise countenance, and a manly garo; his discourse is rational and witty, sober and difercet: But good Lord! how foolishly I talk to him? I never spake duller, nor so senselesly, since I was taught words, and he came purposely, as he told me, to hear me speak, and prove my wit; But it was a sign he heard none, for he grew soon a weary of my company, he staid so short a time: I am troubled often with prating fools, whose visits are as tedious, as their discourses: But

Lord! why do I condemn others, as fools, when this Gentleman, Monsieur Discretion, hath proved me one.

[Exit.

ACT III

SCENE I

Enter **MADAMOSEL CAPRISIA**, and **MONSIEUR IMPORTUNATE**.

MONSIEUR IMPORTUNATE
What? musing by your self, alone! May I question your oughts?

MADAMOSEL CAPRISIA
If you do, you will not be resolved, for there is none at home, to give you an answer.

MONSIEUR IMPORTUNATE
Why, where are they? wandring abroad?

MADAMOSEL CAPRISIA
They like a brood of Birds, are flown out of their Neasts; for thoughts flies with swifter speed, than time can do, having large wings, of quick desire.

MONSIEUR IMPORTUNATE
Faith, you are a great wit!

MADAMOSEL CAPRISIA
You are a great trouble!

[She offers to go forth, He stayes her; She is angry.

MADAMOSEL CAPRISIA
What, you will not force me to stay against my will?

MONSIEUR IMPORTUNATE
Yes, that I will; For your Father saith, you shall be my Wife, and then you will imbrace, and kiss me, as coy as you are now.

MADAMOSEL CAPRISIA
Which if I do, I wish my arms, when they do wind about your waste, may sting as Serpents, and that my kisses may prove poyson to your lips.

MONSIEUR IMPORTUNATE
What, are you seriously angry; Nay, then 'tis time to leave you.

[Exit.

[The **LADY** alone.

MADAMOSEL CAPRISIA
I have heard, that gallant men are civil to our Sex, but I have met with none, but rough, rude, rugged natures, more cruel than wild Tygars.

[Enter **MONSIEUR BON CAMPAIGNON**.

MONSIEUR BON CAMPAIGNON
Why do you complain of our Sex, Lady? what is it you would have?

MADAMOSEL CAPRISIA
I would have a gray-headed wisdom, a middle-aged humour, a fresh mouthed wit, a new bloom'd youth, and a beauty that every one fancies.

MONSIEUR BON CAMPAIGNON
Why, so you have.

MADAMOSEL CAPRISIA
Then I have what I desire.

[She goes out.

MONSIEUR BON CAMPAIGNON
O! She hath a sharp wit, it is vitral wit.

[Exit.

SCENE II

Enter **MADAMOSEL SOLID**, and **MONSIEUR COMORADE**.

MONSIEUR COMORADE
Lady, you have kill'd a Gentleman.

MADAMOSEL SOLID
Who, I! why, I never had the courage to kill a fly.

MONSIEUR COMORADE
You have kill'd him with your disdain.

MADAMOSEL SOLID
I am sorry he had so weak a life, as so slight a cause, as a womans disdain, could destroy it; but for my part, I disdain no man, although I cannot intimately love all men.

MONSIEUR COMORADE

He is but one man, Lady.

MADAMOSEL SOLID

And I have but one particular love to give, or rather I may say, to be gain'd, for I cannot dispose of it; for it will be only disposed by it self, without my leave, so as I must be guided by that which will not be guided by me? I can lend my pity, but not give him my love.

MONSIEUR COMORADE

I suppose you have given him some encouragement, and hopes, if not an assurance, by reason, he sayes, you have forsaken him.

MADAMOSEL SOLID

Not unless common civility, be an encouragement, and ordinary conversation gives hopes; as for an assurance, indeed I gave Monsieur Profession; For I did assure him, I could not love him, as he would have me love him, as Husband. But, O vain man! to brag of that he never had.

MONSIEUR COMORADE

'Tis no brag, Lady, to confess he is forsaken.

MADAMOSEL SOLID

It is a brag, for in that he implyes, he hath been beloved, for the one must be, before the other.

MONSIEUR COMORADE

Pray Madam, let me perswade you, to entertain his love, he is a Gentleman who hath worth, person and wealth, all which he offers you, as to his Goddesse, and a good offer is not to be refused, Lady, when it may lawfully be taken.

MADAMOSEL SOLID

You say true, Sir, and could I perswade my love, as easily as you can commend the man, 'tis likely I should not refuse him.

MONSIEUR COMORADE

But you will be thought cruel, to let a Gentleman dye, for want of your love.

MADAMOSEL SOLID

Why, put the case I have other Lovers, as passionate, and worthy as he; how would you have me divide my self amongst them? Or can you tell me how to please them; I cannot marry them all, the Laws forbids it, and to be the common Mistresse to them, all honour, and honesty forbids it; for though there is some excuse for men, who hath by custom their liberty in amours, because their amours obstructs not nature, so makes breach of honesty; but women are not only barr'd by nature, but custom of subjection, and modesty of education, wherefore, if they should take liberty to several Lovers, or loves courtships, they would not only dishonour themselves, and their whole Sex, and their living friends; but their dishonour would outreach their Posterity, and run back to their Fore-fathers, that were dead long, long before they were born; for their unchaste lives, would be as marks of disgrace, and spots of infamie upon the Tombs of those dead Ancestors, and their ashes would be full'd with their stains, whereas, a chast woman, and a gallant man, obliges both the living, and the dead; for they give honour to their dead Ancestors in their Graves, and to those friends that are living in the World, and to those that shall succeed them; Besides, their examples of their vermes, for all Ages to take out patterns from.

MONSIEUR COMORADE
Madam, you have answered so well, for your self, and Sex, as I can say no more in the behalf of my friend.

[Exit.

SCENE III

Enter **MADAM LA MERE**, and **MADAMOSEL CAPRISIA** her daughter.

MADAM LA MERE
Daughter, your tongue is so sharp, as it is not only poynted, but edged on both sides.

MADAMOSEL CAPRISIA
Use, Mother, will blunt the poynt, and flat the edges.

MADAM LA MERE
No, Daughter, the more 'tis used, the sharper it will be, for words and passions, are the whetstones to that Razor.

MADAMOSEL CAPRISIA
As long as that Razor shaves no reputation, let it raze, or shave, what it will.

[Exit.

SCENE IV.

Enter **MADAMOSEL SOLID, MADAMOSEL DOLTCHE, MADAMOSEL VOLANTE**, and a Grave **MATRON**.

MATRON
Madamosel Solid, what say you to Monsieur Ralleries wit?

MADAMOSEL SOLID
I say of him, as I would of a wild or skittish jade, who hath only strength to kick and fling, but not to travel, or to bear any weight; so Rallerie, is antick postures, and laughing reproaches, not solid and judicious discourses, or continued speeches, the truth is, a ralleying wit, is like obstructed, or corrupted lungs, which causes difficult, and short breathing; So that wit, is short and pussing, spurting out words, questions and replyes; 'tis squib wit, or boys sport

MATRON
Madamosel Doltche, what say you of Monsieur Satericals wit?

MADAMOSEL DOLTCHE
As I would of frosty weather; his wit is sharp, but wholesome, and though he hath a frowning brow, yet he hath a clear soul.

MATRON
Madamosel Volante,
What say you of Monsieur Pedants wit.

MADAMOSEL VOLANTE
As I would of Leeches; for as Leeches sucks bloud from the back parts of men, and spues it forth, when rubb'd with salt; so Monsieur Pedant sucks wit from other mens pens, and mouths, and then spues it sorth again; being rubb'd with the itch of prayse; But all the learned knows, the wit was no more his own, than the bloud that was suck'd, was the Leeches.

MATRON
What say you of Monsieur Lyricks wit?

MADAMOSEL VOLANTE
As I would of a Bird, that chirps more than sings.

MATRON
Madamosel Doltche,
What say you of Monsieur Tragedians wit?

MADAMOSEL DOLTCHE
As I would of Winter, wherein is more rain than Sun-shines, more storms than calms, more night than day; so his wit, hath more melancholly than mirth, causing, or producing tears, sighs and sadnesse; the truth is, his wit dwels in the shades of death.

MATRON
Madamosel Solid, what say you to Monsieur Comicals wit?

MADAMOSEL SOLID
As I would of the Spring, which revives, and refreshes the life of every thing, it is lightsom and gay; So Monsieur Comicals wit is chearfull, pleasant, lively, natural and profitable, as being edifying.

[Exit.

SCENE V

Enter **MADAM LA MERE**, and **MADAMOSEL CAPRISIA**, her Daughter

MADAM LA MERE
Daughter, let me tell you, you have brought your Hogs to a fair Market.

MADAMOSEL CAPRISIA
That is better, than to keep them in a foul stye, Mother.

MADAM LA MERE
You cannot speak without crossing.

MADAMOSEL CAPRISIA
Nor readily crosse without speaking.

MADAM LA MERE
I am sure, your bitter discourses, and crosse answers, hath caused the Lady, namely, the Lady Hercules, to send a rayling message, by a Messenger, to declare her anger for your abusive discourses against her.

MADAMOSEL CAPRISIA
I never mentioned her in my discourse, in my life.

MADAM LA MERE
But you speak against big, and tall women.

MADAMOSEL CAPRISIA
I gave but my opinion of the size, and Sex, not of any particular, and I may speak freely, my opinion of the generalities.

MADAM LA MERE
You may chance, by your opinion of the generalities, to be generally talk'd of.

MADAMOSEL CAPRISIA
Why, then I shall live in discourse, although discourse were dead in me, and who had not rather live, although an ill life, than dye?

MADAM LA MERE
But you might live so, as to gain every bodyes good opinion, if you would palliate your humour, and sweeten your discourse, and endeavour to please in conversation.

MADAMOSEL CAPRISIA
Which do you mean, Mother! either to please my self, or the company?

MADAM LA MERE
Why, the company.

MADAMOSEL CAPRISIA
That is impossible, for in all company, there is diversities, and contrarieties of humours, passions, appetites, delights, pleasures, opinions, judgements, wits, understandings, and the like, and for talking, speaking and discoursing, they are inter-changing, inter-mixing, reasoning, arguing disputing, which causes contradictions, wherefore to agree in, and to every humour, passion, opinion, and discourse, is impossible; indeed one may seemly, or truly agree, and approve of any one opinion or discourse; but not a diversity of discourses, opinions; also one may flatteringly applaud, or sooth any particular persons humour, but not diverse persons, diverse humours, but to flatter, is base, as to approve in their words,

and disapprove in their thoughts, as to commend, or applaud that, or those, that is not praise-worthy: But howsoever, for the soothing of any bodies humour, I will never take the pains, for why should I make my self a slave to the several humours of mankind, who is never in one humour two minutes, and why may not I think, or desire to be flattered, and humoured, as well as others, and when I am not flattered, and humoured, to be as much displeased at others, as others at me: Wherefore, good Mother, be not you displeased, that I chose rather to displease my self, than any body else, besides your self.

MADAM LA MERE
You will follow your own wayes, Daughter.

MADAMOSEL CAPRISIA
I cannot walk safer, than in my own ground, Mother.

[Exit.

SCENE VI

Enter **MONSIEUR PERFECTION**, and **MADAMOSEL SOLID**.

MONSIEUR PERFECTION
Dear Mistress, I fear my absence hath made you forget me.

MADAMOSEL SOLID
No certainly, I cannot forget you, by reason my brain is hung about with the memory of your worthy nature, and meritorious actions; which my love doth admire, and takes delight for to view each several piece and part.

MONSIEUR PERFECTION
Do you love me?

MADAMOSEL SOLID
How can I chose but love, when in my infancy, such a number of words, in your praise, was thrown into my ears, like seeds into the Earth, which took root in my heart, from which love sprouted forth, and grew up with my years.

MONSIEUR PERFECTION
And will you be constant?

MADAMOSEL SOLID
As day is to the Sun!

MONSIEUR PERFECTION
Do you speak truth?

MADAMOSEL SOLID

Truly, I have been bred up so much, and so long, in the wayes of truth, as I know no tract of dissembling; and therefore, certainly, my words will ever keep within the compass of Truth, and my actions will alwaies turn, and run with that byas, but why do you seem to doubt, in making such questions.

MONSIEUR PERFECTION
I will truly confess, I have heard, that since I have been in the Countrey, you had entertained another Lover.

MADAMOSEL SOLID
It's false, but false reports, is like breathing upon a pure and clear Glasse, it dimns it for a time; but that malicious breath, soon vanishes, and leaves no stain behind it; so I hope your jealousie will do the like, it will vanish, and leave no doubt behind it.

MONSIEUR PERFECTION
I hope you are not angry with me, for telling you, or for being my self troubled, at what was reported.

MADAMOSEL SOLID
No, for innocency is never concern'd, it always lives in peace and quiet, having a satisfaction in it self, wherefore reports only siezes on the guilty, arresting them with an angry turbulency.

MONSIEUR PERFECTION
But, perchance you may be angry for my jealousie.

MADAMOSEL SOLID
No, for jealousie expresses love, as being affraid to lose, what it desires to keep.

MONSIEUR PERFECTION
Then, I hope you do not repent the love you have placed on me.

MADAMOSEL SOLID
Heaven may sooner repent of doing good, than I repent my love and choyce.

MONSIEUR PERFECTION
Dear Mistress, my mind is so full of joy, since it is clear'd of suspition, and assured of your love, as my thoughts doth fly about my brain, like birds in Sun-shine weather.

[Exit.

SCENE VII

Enter **MONSIEUR NOBILISSIMO**, and **MADAMOSEL DOLTCHE**.

MONSIEUR NOBILISSIMO
Sweet Lady, will you give me leave to be your Servant!

MADAMOSEL DOLTCHE

I wish I were a Mistress worthy of your service.

MONSIEUR NOBILISSIMO
There is no man shall admire more your beauty, and wit, nor be more diligent to your youth, nor shall honour your merits, and love your vertue more than I.

MADAMOSEL DOLTCHE
Indeed, I had rather be honoured for my merit, than for my birth, for my breeding, than for my wealth, and I had rather be beloved for my vertue, than admired for my beauty; and I had rather be commended for my silence, than for my wit.

MONSIEUR NOBILISSIMO
It were pity you should bury your great wit in silence.

MADAMOSEL DOLTCHE
My wit is according to my years, tender and young.

MONSIEUR NOBILISSIMO
Your wit, Lady, may entertain the silver haired Sages.

MADAMOSEL DOLTCHE
No surely, for neither my years, nor my wit, are arrived to that degree, as to make a good companion, having had neither the experience of time, nor practice of speech; for I have been almost a mute hitherto, and a stranger to the World.

MONSIEUR NOBILISSIMO
The World is wide, and to travel in it, is both dangerous and difficult; wherefore, you being young, should take a guide, to protect and direct you, and there is no Guide nor Protector so honourable, and safe, as a Husband; what think you of marriage.

MADAMOSEL DOLTCHE
Marriage, and my thoughts, live at that distance, as they seldom meet.

MONSIEUR NOBILISSIMO
Why, I hope you have not made a vow, to live a single life.

MADAMOSEL DOLTCHE
No, for the Laws of Morality, and Divinity, are chains, which doth sufficiently restrain mankind, and tyes him into a narrow compasse; and though I will not break those chaining Laws, to get lose, and so become lawless; yet I will not tye nature harder with vain opinions, and unnecessary vows, than she is tyed already.

MONSIEUR NOBILISSIMO
You shall need no Tutour, for you cannot only instruct your self, but teach others.

MADAMOSEL DOLTCHE

Alas, my brain is like unplanted ground, and my words like wild fruits, or like unprofitable grain, that yields no nourishing food to the understanding; Wherefore, if I should offer to speak, my speech must be to ask questions, not to give instructions.

MONSIEUR NOBILISSIMO
Certainly, Lady, nature did study the architectour of your form, and drew from herself the purest extractions, for your mind, and your soul, the essence or spirits of those extractions, or rather you appear to me, a miracle, something above nature, to be so young and beautifull, and yet so vertuous, witty and wise, grac'd with such civil behaviour; for many a grave beard, would have wagg'd with talking, lesse sense, with more words.

MADAMOSEL DOLTCHE
Youth and age, is subject to errors, one for want of time to get experience, the other through long time, wherein they lose their memory.

MONSIEUR NOBILISSIMO
Pray let me get your affections, and then I shall not lose my hopes of a vertuous Lady to my wife.

[Exit.

SCENE VIII

Enter **MADAMOSEL CAPRISIA**, and **MONSIEUR GENEROSITY**.

MONSIEUR GENEROSITY
Lady, are you walking studiously alone? may I not be thought rude, if I should ask what your studies are?

MADAMOSEL CAPRISIA
I am studying, how some studies for pain, some pleasure, some dangers, some quarrels, some to be wicked, some to be learned, some to be ignorant, some to be foolish, some to be famous, but few to be wise.

MONSIEUR GENEROSITY
Who studies to be wicked?

MADAMOSEL CAPRISIA
Thieves, Murtherers, Adulterers, Lyers, and Extortioners.

MONSIEUR GENEROSITY
Who studies to be learned?

MADAMOSEL CAPRISIA
Linguists.

MONSIEUR GENEROSITY
Who studies to be ignorant?

MADAMOSEL CAPRISIA
Divines.

MONSIEUR GENEROSITY
Who studies quarrels?

MADAMOSEL CAPRISIA
Lawyers.

MONSIEUR GENEROSITY
Who studies dangers?

MADAMOSEL CAPRISIA
Souldiers.

MONSIEUR GENEROSITY
Who studies to be fools?

MADAMOSEL CAPRISIA
Buffoones.

MONSIEUR GENEROSITY
Who studies fame?

MADAMOSEL CAPRISIA
Poets.

MONSIEUR GENEROSITY
Who studies pleasure?

MADAMOSEL CAPRISIA
Epicures.

MONSIEUR GENEROSITY
Who studies pain?

MADAMOSEL CAPRISIA
Epicures.

MONSIEUR GENEROSITY
Do Epicures study both for pain, and pleasure?

MADAMOSEL CAPRISIA
Yes, for they that surfeit with pleasure, must endure pain; and Epicures studies the height of pleasure, which no sooner injoyed, but pain follows.

MONSIEUR GENEROSITY

Who studies to be wise?

MADAMOSEL CAPRISIA
They that study Temperance, Prudence, Fortitude and Justice.

MONSIEUR GENEROSITY
And, what study you?

MADAMOSEL CAPRISIA
I study how I may avoid the company of mankind, also, to be quit of your Lordships presence.

[He alone. She goeth out.

MONSIEUR GENEROSITY
She is so handsome, no humour can ill become her.

[Exit.

SCENE IX

Enter **MONSIEUR PROFESSION**, and **MONSIEUR COMORADE**.

MONSIEUR COMORADE
Thom. Give me leave to rejoyce with thee, for the resurrection of thy heart, that was kill'd with thy Mistresses cruelty, and buried in her constancy.

MONSIEUR PROFESSION
Well, well? make your self merry.

MONSIEUR COMORADE
But prethee, in what plight is thy heart? I doubt it is lean, weak and pale, and in a puling condition, lying in the Grave of thy Mistresses inconstancy.

MONSIEUR PROFESSION
Faith, I cannot tell; the good Angel that brought into life, can give a better account of it, than I can.

MONSIEUR COMORADE
Where shall I seek this good Angel? amongst the effeminate or masculine Sex: For I suppose, it is an Angel that is of one Sex, although I have heard, Angels are of neither Sex; but prethee, of which shall I inquire.

MONSIEUR PROFESSION
Of the divine Sex, and the divinest of her Sex.

MONSIEUR COMORADE

You may as well bid me inquire of that which is not to be found, for every particular man that is a Servant to any particular of these angelical creatures, will prefer his own Mistress, to be the divinest, and so the most absolutest.

MONSIEUR PROFESSION
All men that sees my Mistresse, and doth not adore her, as the only She, is damned in ignorance, and condemned to perpetual blindnesse.

MONSIEUR COMORADE
Say you so, then I will not see her, for fear I should be one of the damned, and therefore I will give over that design, as the search of her, and go to a Tavern, and drink the good health of thy heart, and leave the inquiry after it, and if you will go with me, so.

MONSIEUR PROFESSION
I cannot, without the breach of gratitude, deny thy kindnesse; wherefore, I will bear thee company.

[Exit.

SCENE X

Enter **DOCTOR FREEDOM**, and **MADAMOSEL DOLTCHE, MADAMOSEL SOLID, MADAMOSEL VOLANTE.**

MADAMOSEL SOLID
O, you are welcome, Doctor Freedom.

DOCTOR FREEDOM
If I be not welcome now, I shall never be welcome.

MADAMOSEL VOLANTE
Why, Doctor? what Present have you brought us? that can make you so acceptable, is it perpetual youth, or undeniable beauty, or everlasting life? But prethee, Doctor, what is it that will make thee so welcome?

DOCTOR FREEDOM
Why, my self; here being so many young Ladies together, and not a man amongst them.

MADAMOSEL VOLANTE
Thy self, Doctor! why, thou art not worth the dregs of an Urinal, of a sick water, if it were not for our charity, and generosity, more than thy merit, ability or service, you would have but a cold entertainment, and a rule welcome.

DOCTOR FREEDOM
Well, my young, wity, saterycal Patient, you will take a surfeit of fruit, milk, puddings, pyes, or sweet-meats, one of these dayes, and then you will flatter me.

MADAMOSEL VOLANTE

You say right, Doctor; but now I speak truth, and is not that better than to flatter, or dissemble; For there is none but sick, and deprav'd souls, that will deliver Truth with a quarter, half, or three quartred face, like Merchants, or mechanick, that would sell off their ill commodities, with a broken light, but a noble and healthfull soul, shews the full face of Truth, in a clear light; wherefore, the sick and base, will flatter, but the noble and free, will speak truth.

DOCTOR FREEDOM
Well, I am sure you think better of me in your thoughts, than your words expresses.

MADAMOSEL VOLANTE
Let me tell you, my words and thoughts, are so well acquainted, as they never dissemble, and there is such a friendship betwixt them, as they never move several wayes, but runs even together: But let me tell thee, Doctor, I have such a spleen to thy Sex, as I desire to kill them, at least, to wound them with spitefull words; and I wish I had beauty enough for to damn them, causing them to be perjured, by forsaking other women, they were bound by sacred vows, and holy bonds.

[Enter **MONSIEUR DISCRETION**.

MONSIEUR DISCRETION
It is well, Master Doctor, that you can be priviledg'd amongst the young Ladyes, at all times, when such as I, that have not your Profession, are oftentimes shut, and lockt out.

DOCTOR FREEDOM
Faith, if you have no better entertainment, than I have had since I came, it were better you were from them, than with them, for their tongues are as sharp as needles.

MADAMOSEL VOLANTE
'Tis a sign we want work, when we are forc'd to stitch our wit upon you.

MONSIEUR DISCRETION
How dare you anger the Doctor, when your life lyes upon his skill.

MADAMOSEL VOLANTE
O! His skill lyes upon chance, and it is a chance, whether he kills, or cures, is it not, Doctor?

DOCTOR FREEDOM
No, for I can kill my Patients, when I will, although not cure them, when I will.

MADAMOSEL VOLANTE
Well, then, Doctor, when I would dye, I will send for you, but not when I would live.

MONSIEUR DISCRETION
Your Servant, Ladies.

[**MONSIEUR DISCRETION** goeth out.

DOCTOR FREEDOM

Good Lady Wit, follow Monsieur Discretion, he will make you a wise Lady, and make your wit discreet, as it should be.

MADAMOSEL VOLANTE
O Doctor! how you mistake, for wit cannot be made, it is a Creator, and not a Creature; for wit was the first Master, or Mistress of Arts; the first Husband-man, Granger, Gardiner, Carver, Painter, Graver, Caster and Moulder, Mason, Joyner Smith, Brasier, Glazier, the first Chandler, Vintener, Brewer, Baker, Cook, Confectioner, the first Spinster, Weaver, Knitter, Tayler, Shoo-maker, and millions the like; also wit was the first Navigator, Architector, Mathematician, Logitian, Geometrician, Cosmografir, Astronomer, Astrologer, Philosopher, Poet, Historian and Hearold; also wit made the first Common-wealth, invented Laws for Peace, Arms for Wars, Ceremonies for State and Religion; also musick, dancing, dressing, masking, playing for delight and pleasure; wit divides time, imployes time, prevents time, and provides for time; it makes Heavens, and Hells, Gods and Divels.

DOCTOR FREEDOM
Well, go thy wayes, for though thou hast a heavenly mind, and an angelical beauty, yet thou hast a devilish wit,

MADAMOSEL VOLANTE
It shall be sure to torment thee, Doctor, but do you hear, Doctor? pray present my service to Monsieur Discretion, and tell him, it was a signe he lik'd not our company, he made so short a stay.

DOCTOR FREEDOM
He perceived by your usage of me, that if he stayd, you would beat him out of your company, with your two edged tongues; but I will tell him what a Rallery you are.

MADAMOSEL VOLANTE
I hope you will give me a good report, for I have fully charged you.

DOCTOR FREEDOM
You have over-charged me, and therefore it is likely I shall break into exclamations.

[Exit.

ACT IV

SCENE I

Enter **MONSIEUR IMPORTUNATE**, and **MADAMOSEL CAPRISIA**.

MONSIEUR IMPORTUNATE
Lady, if I may not be your Husband, pray let there be a friendship between us?

MADAMOSEL CAPRISIA

What kind of friendship would you make? for there are so many, and of such different natures, as I know not which you would be; as some friendship is made by beauty, some by flattery, some by luxurie, some by factions, others by knavery, and all for interest.

MONSIEUR IMPORTUNATE
None for love?

MADAMOSEL CAPRISIA
No, but some are made by lust, but they last not long.

MONSIEUR IMPORTUNATE
And is there no friendship made by vertue?

MADAMOSEL CAPRISIA
O no, for vertue may walk all the World over, and meet never a friend, which is the cause she lives alone; for all the World thinks her too rigid for Society, which makes mankind adhere to her enemie vice.

MONSIEUR IMPORTUNATE
Doth not marriage make a friendship?

MADAMOSEL CAPRISIA
Very seldom, for marriage is like a Common-wealth, which is a contract of bodyes, or rather a contract of interest, not a friendship betwixt souls, and there is as much Faction, and oftener civil Wars in marriage, than in publick Common-wealths.

MONSIEUR IMPORTUNATE
I desire our friendship may be Platonick.

MADAMOSEL CAPRISIA
That is too dangerous, for it oftimes proves a Traytor to Chastity.

[Exit.

SCENE II

Enter **MONSIEUR NOBILISSIMO, MADAMOSEL DOLTCHE**, and her **NURSE**.

NURSE
Sir, you must give me leave to chide you, for staying so long with my Nurse-child, as you keep her from her dinner, either go away, or stay and dine with her.

MONSIEUR NOBILISSIMO
Good Nurse, be patient, for though I am engaged to dine with other company; yet her discourse is such charming musick, as I have not power to go from her, as yet.

MADAMOSEL DOLTCHE
If my discourse sounds musical, 'tis only when you are by, but when you are absent, the strings of my voice, or speech, is as if they were broken, for then my tongue is out of Tune, and my wit is out of humour.

MONSIEUR NOBILISSIMO
My dearest and sweetest Mistress, may your merits be rewarded by Fame, your vertue by Heaven, your life by Nature, and all your earthly desires by Fortune.

MADAMOSEL DOLTCHE
And my love by the return of yours:

MONSIEUR NOBILISSIMO
When I forsake you, may Hell take my soul, and Divels torment it for ingratitude and perjury.

[Exit.

SCENE III

Enter **MADAMOSEL VOLANTE**, and a Grave **MATRON**.

MATRON
Madamosel Doltche seems to be a very fine, sweet Lady, well-behav'd, sober, modest, discreet, and of a gentle nature.

MADAMOSEL VOLANTE
Most commonly, every one seems best at the first sight, by reason they put on their civilest demeanors, gracefullest garbs, modestest countenance, and speaks their most choycest phrases, or words, when they meet strangers; all which, makes them appear to their advantage, when after acquantaince, they will seem but vulgar, as when they are used to their ordinary garbs, countenances and phrases, and that their natures and dispositions were known, they will appear to be no better than their Neighbours; nay, perchance not so good; the like will Madamosel Doltche appear to you.

MATRON
I do suppose she looks more familiar on her acquaintance, than strangers, and it is likely, she looks more grave, and sober on strangers, than on her known friends, and familiars; yet those several looks and countenances, may be as pleasing, and obliging, the one, as the other; for though the one may be more kind, the other may be more respectfull; for every ones countenance and behaviour, is to be ordered according to the several degrees or relations of several persons, and to several persons, and to several sexes, or according to their condition, state, life and fortune, and according to the times and occasions; for women are, or should be, more free and confident to, and in the company of women, than men; and men are more respectfull in their discourse and behaviour to women, than to their own Sex, and a merry countenance in a sad condition or state of life or fortunes, would not be seemly; mirth in the house of mourning, would be inhumane, or to dance or sing over the Graves of their Parents, Children, Husbands, Wives or Friends, would be unnatural, or to be merry in the time of a general calamity, as in timate of Wars, Plagues, or Pamine, or Deluges, or to be sad or froward in a general rejoycing; but a sad

countenance, and a grave behaviour, is as sitting, and seems comely and handsome in a time of calamity, as a merry countenance, and a dancing behaviour, in a time of rejoycing; for tears becomes the face, sometimes, as well as smiles, and blushing may appear and expresse a modest nature to strangers, when to familiar acquaintantances, blushing might be thought an accuser, or witnesse of some crime, yet bashfull eyes at all times, becomes modest Virgins.

MADAMOSEL VOLANTE
I hate bashfull eyes, for they are like to troubled waters, thick and unsteady, rouling from place to place, without an assurance; for modest Virgins may look upon the World with a confident brow, if they have no guilt to stain their cheeks with blushes, and surely amongst well-brod persons, there is none so rude, injurious, or uncivil, to force the bloud to rise, or stop the light, in causing bashfull eyes, but such as condemns a confident countenance in Virgins faces; my eye of understanding will cast a despising glance on such ridiculous fools, and the tongue of reason condemns them.

[Exit.

SCENE IV

Enter **MADAM LA MERE**, and **MADAMOSEL CAPRISIA** her daughter.

MADAM LA MERE
I wonder, Daughter, you should be so rudely uncivil to Monsieur Generosity, to use him so unkindly, as to entertain him with scornfull words, and disrespectfull behaviour.

MADAMOSEL CAPRISIA
Why did he come to visit me?

MADAM LA MERE
To offer his service, and to professe his affection to your person and vertue.

MADAMOSEL CAPRISIA
I care not for his service, or affection.

MADAM LA MERE
But he is a person of an honourable Title, and can make you a great Lady.

MADAMOSEL CAPRISIA
Give me leave to tell you, Mother, that nature hath given me Titles of Honour, Wit and Beauty, to which all men will bow to, with respect; Titles from Kings, poor petty things to those.

MADAM LA MERE
But Daughter, let me tell you, that wit and beauty, without modesty, civility and vertuous courtesie, may insnare facile fools, and allure fond persons, but not perswade the judicious to esteem you, nor the constant to sue to you, nor true love to desire you; you may have vain Boasters, and amotous Flatterers to court you; but none that is wise, or honourable, will marry you, and to use this Noble Lord so

disrespectfully, who is indued with vertue, and adorned with the graces, and beloved of the Muses, is a crime unpardonable.

MADAMOSEL CAPRISIA
Mother, the Muses and the Graces are Witches, which enchants the soul, and charms the Spirits, and makes the Senses extravagant, and the actions desperate.

MADAM LA MERE
Methinks they should charm you; if they have such power.

MADAMOSEL CAPRISIA
My humour is a Spell against all such charms.

[Exit.

SCENE V

Enter **MONSIEUR PROFESSION**, and **MONSIEUR COMORADE** his Friend.

MONSIEUR COMORADE
You are well met, for I was going to your lodging to see you.

MONSIEUR PROFESSION
And I am now going home, and therefore let us go together.

MONSIEUR COMORADE
Where have you been?

MONSIEUR PROFESSION
At a house you often resort to.

MONSIEUR COMORADE
What, at a Bawdy-house?

MONSIEUR PROFESSION
Yes.

MONSIEUR COMORADE
Why, how durst you venture?

MONSIEUR PROFESSION
Why?

MONSIEUR COMORADE
Why! why if your angelical Mistresse should come to hear of it; Faith, she would bury your heart again.

MONSIEUR PROFESSION
Yes, is it were not out of her power.

MONSIEUR COMORADE
Why, hath she not the Possession?

MONSIEUR PROFESSION
No saith.

MONSIEUR COMORADE
How comes that to passe?

MONSIEUR PROFESSION
I know not how, but upon some dislike, it grew weary, and by some opportunity, it found it stole home, and since it hath promised never to leave me again; for it hath confessed to me, it hath been most miserably tormented with doubts, fears, jealousies and despairs.

MONSIEUR COMORADE
Prethee let me tell thee, as a friend, that thy heart, is a false lying heart, for there inhabits no torments amongst angelical bodies.

MONSIEUR PROFESSION
By your favour, in Plutoes Court, there be Angels as well, and as many as in loves; But let me tell you, that if I did not love you very well, I would call you to an account, for calling my heart, a false lying heart.

MONSIEUR COMORADE
Prethee pacifie thy self, for I am sure I have had but a heartless friend of thee, all the time of thy hearts absence, and if I should rayle of thy heart, thou hast no reason to condemn me; but prethee, tell me, had not thy heart some pleasure sometimes to mitigate the torments?

MONSIEUR PROFESSION
No saith, for my heart tells me, that what with rigid vertue, cruel scorn, and insulting pride, it never had a minutes pleasure, nor so much as a moment of ease; and if that there were no more hopes of happiness amongst the Gods in Heaven, than there is amongst the Goddesses on Earth, it would never desire to go to them, or dwell amongst them: Nay, my heart says, it should be as much affraid to go to Heaven, and to be with the Gods, as mortals are to go to Hell, to be with Divels.

MONSIEUR COMORADE
But if pleasure, and happiness, is not to be found with vertue, nor with the Gods, where shall we seek for it.

MONSIEUR PROFESSION
I will tell you what my heart saith, and doth assure me; that is, that pleasure lives alwaies with vice, and that good fellowship is amongst the damned, and it doth swear, it is a most melancholly life, to live with those that are called the blessed, which are the Goddesses on Earth.

MONSIEUR COMORADE
Why, then let us return to the house from whence you came.

MONSIEUR PROFESSION
No faith, I am dry, wherefore I will go to a Tavern.

MONSIEUR COMORADE
Content.

[Exit.

SCENE VI

Enter **MADAMOSEL CAPRISIA** alone, in a studeous humour, walking for a time silently; then speaks.

MADAMOSEL CAPRISIA
Which shall I complain of? Nature or Education; I am compassionate by nature; for though I am froward, I am not cruel, I am pious by education; for though I am froward, I am not wicked, I am vertuous by nature, and education; for though I am froward, I am neither dishonest, unchaste, base, or unworthy: Why then, 'tis Fortune I must complain of, for Fortune hath given me plenty, and plenty hath made me proud, and pride hath made me self-conceited, self-conceit hath bred disdain, and disdain scorn; So pride, disdain, and scorn, makes me disapprove all other creatures actions, or opinions, but my own; and this disapproving is that which men calls cross, pievish, and froward disposition, being most commonly, accompanied with sharp satyrical words, and angry frowns.
These faults i'l conquer, whereresoere they lye;
I'l rule my froward humour, or i'l dye.

[Exit.

SCENE VII

Enter **MADAMOSEL SOLID**, and a **MATRON**.

MADAMOSEL SOLID
Lord! Lord! I wonder men and women should spend their time so idley, and wast their lives so vainly, in talking so ignorantly, and acting so foolishly upon the great Stage, or the Stage of the great World.

MATRON
Why, how would you have them spend their time, or talk, or act?

MADAMOSEL SOLID
I would have them spend their time, to gain time, as to prevent or hinder times oblivion, and to speak and act to that design,
That when their bodies dye,
Their Names and Fames, may live eternally.

MATRON
But it is not in every mans, or womans power, to get same, for some are made uncapable by nature, others are hindred by fortune, some are obstructed by chance, others want time and opportunity, wealth, birth and education, and many that are pull'd back by envie, spite and malice.

MADAMOSEL SOLID
What man or woman soever, that nature is liberal to, may eternalize themselves; as for fortune, she may hinder the active, the like may chance, envie, spite and malice, but cannot hinder the contemplative; the like may time and opportunity; but poor poverty and birth, can be no hindrance to natural wit, for natural wit, in a poor Cottage, may spin an afterlife, enter-weaving several colour'd fancies, and threeds of opinions, making fine and curious Tapestries to hang in the Chambers of fame, or wit may and carve Images of imaginations, to place and set forth the Gardens of fame, making fountains of Poetry, that may run in smooth streams of verse, or wit may paint and pensel out some Copies, and various Pictures of Nature, with the pensels of Rhethorick on the grounds of Philosophy, to hang in the Galleries of fame; Thus the Palacesses of fame may be furnished and adorn'd by the wit of a poor Cottager.

[Exit.

SCENE VIII

Enter **MADAMOSEL CAPRISIA**, sola.

MADAMOSEL CAPRISIA
Item, I am to be courteous, but not familiar; to be merry, but not wild; to be kind, but not wanton, to be friendly, but not intimate; to be sociable, but not troublesome; to be conversable, but not talkative; to look soberly, but not frowningly; to return answers civilly, to ask questions wisely, to demand rights honestly, to argue rationally, and to maintain opinions probably: These rules I will strictly observe, and constantly practice.

[Enter **MONSIEUR BON CAMPAIGNON**.

MADAMOSEL CAPRISIA
Sir, I cry peccavi, and ask your pardon, for speaking so unhandsomely of the effeminate Sex, when I was last in your company; for my indiscretion made me forget, so as not to remember, that all men hath either Wives, Sisters, Daughters or Mothers: But truly, my discourse proceeded neither from spite or malice, but from the consideration of my own faults, which being so many, did bury the good graces of other women, for though I am vertuously honest, yet I am but rudely fashion'd, and untoward for conversation; but though my discourse had a triangular countenance, for it seem'd foolish, spi•efull and wicked; yet pray, Sir, believe, the natural face, was a perfect, round, honest face.

MONSIEUR BON CAMPAIGNON
Lady, what faults soever, your Sex is guilty of, your vertues will get their pardon, and your beauty will cover their blemishes.

MADAMOSEL CAPRISIA

I wish my indiscretion had not discovered my froward imperfections, but I am sorry, and shall hereafter endeavor to rectifie my errours.

[Exit.

SCENE IX

Enter **MONSIEUR NOBILISSIMO**, and **NURSE**.

MONSIEUR NOBILISSIMO
Good Nurse, where is my vertuous, sweet Mistresse?

NURSE
In her chamber, Sir.

MONSIEUR NOBILISSIMO
What is she doing?

NURSE
She is reading.

MONSIEUR NOBILISSIMO
What Books doth she read? are they Divinity, Morality, Philosophy, History or Poetry?

NURSE
Sometimes her study is of one, and then of another; But now I think, her chief study, is you, wherein she may read humanity.

[Enter **MADAMOSEL DOLTCHE**, and seeing **MONSIEUR NOBILISSIMO** with her **NURSE**, starts back, and then comes forth blushing.

NURSE
Lord child! what makes you blush?

MADAMOSEL DOLTCHE
Not crimes, but my blushing, is caused by a sudden assault, or surprisal meeting him; I did not expect to meet at this time, which raised up blushes in my face; for blushing is like the full and falling tide; for the bloud flows to the face, and from thence ebbes to the heart, as passions moves the mind;
And thoughts as waves, in curling folds do rise,
And lashfull eyes, are like the troubled skies.

MONSIEUR NOBILISSIMO
Sweet Mistress, crimes cannot stain your cheeks with blushes, but modesty hath penseld Roses there, which seems as sweet, as they look fair.

MADAMOSEL DOLTCHE

I desire my looks and countenance, may alwaies appear so, as they may never falsly accuse me; and as I would not have my looks, or countenance, wrong my innocency, or deceive the Spectators, so I would not have my heart be ungratefull to bury your presence in silence; Wherefore, I give you thanks, Sir, for the noble Present you sent me to day.

MONSIEUR NOBILISSIMO
I was affraid you would not have accepted of it.

MADAMOSEL DOLTCHE
Truly, I shall refuse no Present you shall send me, although it were ushered with scorn, and attended with death.

MONSIEUR NOBILISSIMO
My kind Mistress, I shall never send you any Present, but what is ushered by my love, attended by my service, and presented with the offer of my life.

NURSE
Child, you are very free of kind words.

MADAMOSEL DOLTCHE
And my deeds shall answer my words, is need requires; yet I am sorry if my speaking over-much, should offend; but I chose rather, to set bosses of words on the sense of my discourse, although it obscures the glosse of my speech, than my love should be buried in my silence.

MONSIEUR NOBILISSIMO
Sweet Mistresse, your loving expressions gives such joy unto my heart, and such delight unto my hearing, as my soul is inthron'd in happinesse, and crown'd with tranquility.

NURSE
Pray Heaven, you both may be as full of Love, Joy and Peace, when you are married, as you express to have now; But let me tell you, young Lovers, that Hymen is a very temperate, and discreet Gentleman in love, I will assure you; neither doth he expresse himself in such high poetical Raptures, for his discourse is plain, and ordinary.

MONSIEUR NOBILISSIMO
Nay, sometimes his discourse is extraordinary, as when he hath Wars; but Nurse, thou art old, and the fire of love, if ever thou hadst any, is put out by old Father Times extinguisher.

MADAMOSEL DOLTCHE
True love never dyes, nor can time put it out.

MONSIEUR NOBILISSIMO
'Tis true, but Nurse seems by her speech, as if she had never known true love; for true love, as it alwaies burns clear, so it alwaies flames high, far infinite is the fewel that feeds it.

NURSE
Well, well? young Lovers, be not so confident, but let me advise you to ballance reason on both sides, with hopes, and doubts, and then the judgement will be steady.

MONSIEUR NOBILISSIMO
But in the scales of love, Nurse, nothing must be but confidence.

NURSE
Yes, there must be temperance, or love will surfeit, and dye with excess.

MADAMOSEL DOLTCHE
Love cannot surfeit, no more than souls with grace, or Saints of Heaven.

[Exit.

SCENE X

Enter **MADAMOSEL CAPRISIA**, sola.

MADAMOSEL CAPRISIA
My smiles shall be as Baits, my eyes as Angels, where every look shall be a hook to catch a heart; I'l teach my tongue such art, to plant words on each heart, as they shall take deep root, from whence pure love shall spring; my lips shall be as flowery banks, whereon sweet Rhethorick grows, and cipherous fancy blows; from which banks, love shall wish to gather Posies of kisses, where every single kisse shall differ as Roses, Pinks, Violets, Primroses, and Daffidillies, and the breath therefrom, shall be as fragant as the touch, soft thereon, and as the Sun doth heat the Earth, so shall my imbraces heat my Lovers thoughts with self-conceit, which were before like water, frozen with a dejected and despairing cold. Hay ho!

[Exit.

ACT V

SCENE I

Enter **MONSIEUR PROFESSION**, and **MADAMOSEL SOLID**.

MONSIEUR PROFESSION
Dear Mistress, you are the only She that is fit to be crown'd; the sole Empresse of the World.

MADAMOSEL SOLID
Let me tell you, Sir? I had rather be a single Shepheardesse, than the sole Empress of the World; for I would not be a Mistress of so much power, to be as a Servant to so much trouble.

MONSIEUR PROFESSION
But, put the case Alexander were alive, and would crown you Empress of the World, you would not refuse that honour, but accept of it, for the sake of renown.

MADAMOSEL SOLID

Yes, I should refuse it, for if I could not get renown by my own merits, I should wish to dye in Oblivion, for I care not; Nay, I despise such honours and renowns, as comes by derivations, as being deriv'd from another, and not inherent in my self, and it is a poor, and mean renown, that is gain'd or got, only by receiving a gift from a fellow-creature, who gives out of passion, appetite, partiality, vain-glory, or fear, and not for merit or worthsake; wherefore, no gifts but those that comes from the Gods, or Nature, are to be esteem'd, or received with thanks, but were to be refused, had man the power to chose, or to deny.

MONSIEUR PROFESSION

Sweet Mistress, nature hath crown'd you with beauty and wit, and the Gods hath given you a noble soul.

MADAMOSEL SOLID

I wish they had, for the Gods gifts are not like to mans, and natures crown is beyond the golden crown of Art, which are greater glories, than Power, Wealth, Title or Birth, or all the outward honours gain'd on Earth; but I desire the Gods may crown my soul with reason and understanding; Heaven crown my mind with Temperance and Fortitude; Nature crown my body with Health and Strength, time crown my life with comely and discreet age; Death crown my separation with peace and rest; and Fame crown my memory with an everlasting renown; thus may my creation be to a happy end.

MONSIEUR PROFESSION

Gods, Fortune and Fates hath joyned to make me happy in your love, and that which will make me absolutely happy, is, that I shall marry you, and imbrace you as my wife.

MADAMOSEL SOLID

The absolute happiness is, when the Gods imbraces man with mercy, and kisses him with love.

[Exit.

SCENE II

Enter **MADAMOSEL CAPRISIA**.

MADAMOSEL CAPRISIA

Hay, ho! who can love, and be wise? but why do I say so? For reason loves wisely; 'tis only the mistaken senses that loves foolishly; indeed, the sense doth not love, but sondly, and foolishly affects, for it, 'tis an humoursome and inconstant appetite that proceeds from the body, and not that noble passion of true love which proceeds from the soul: But O! what a ridiculous humour am I fallen into, from a cholerick humour, into an amorous humour; Oh! I could tear my soul from my body, for having such whining thoughts, and such a mean, submissive, croaching, feigning, flattering humour, and idle mind; a cholerick humour, is noble to this, for it is commanding, and seems of an heroick spirit, but to be amorous, is base, beastly, and of an inconstant nature.
Oh! How apt is busie life to go amisse,
What foolish humours in mans mind there is:

But O! The soul is far beyond the mind,
As much as man is from the beastly kind.

[Exit.

SCENE III

Enter **MADAMOSEL VOLANTE**, and **DOCTOR FREEDOM**.

DOCTOR FREEDOM
Are you weary of, your life? that you send me; for you said, you would not send for me, untill you had a desire to dye.

MADAMOSEL VOLANTE
True, Doctor, and if you cannot cure me, kill me.

DOCTOR FREEDOM
In my conscience, you have sent for me to play the wanton.

MADAMOSEL VOLANTE
Why, Doctor? If I do not infringe the rules and laws of modesty, or civility, I cannot commit wanton faults,

DOCTOR FREEDOM
Yes faith, your tongue may play the wanton,

MADAMOSEL VOLANTE
Indeed, Doctor, I had rather tell a wanton truth, than a modest lye.

DOCTOR FREEDOM
Well, what is your disease?

MADAMOSEL VOLANTE
Nay, that you must guesse, I can only tell my pains.

DOCTOR FREEDOM
Where is your pain?

MADAMOSEL VOLANTE
In my heart and head.

DOCTOR FREEDOM
Those be dangerous parts, but after what manner are your pains?

MADAMOSEL VOLANTE

On my heart there lyes a weight, as heavy as the World on Atlas shoulders; and from my melancholly mind, arises such damps of doubts, as almost quenches out the fire of life, did not some hope, though weak, which blows with fainting breath, keep it alive, or rather puffs than blows, which intermitting motions, makes my pulse unequal, and my bloud to ebbe and flow, as from my heart, unto my face; and from my face, unto my heart again; as for my head, it feels drousie, and my spirits are dull; my thoughts uneasily doth run, crossing, and striving to throw each other down; this causes broken sleeps, and frightfull dreams, and when I awake at every noyse, I start with fears, my limbs doth shake.

DOCTOR FREEDOM
Why, this disease is love, wherefore I cannot cure you; for love no more than wit, can neither be temper'd, nor yet be rul'd, for love and wit, keeps neither moderate bounds, nor spares diet, but dyes most commonly of a surfeit.

MADAMOSEL VOLANTE
O yes, discretion can cure both.

DOCTOR FREEDOM
Then send for Monsieur Discretion, and hear what he sayes to you, for your disease is past my skil.

MADAMOSEL VOLANTE
By your industry, Doctor, help may be found, in giving directions, and ordering the cordial.

DOCTOR FREEDOM
So I understand you would have my counsel what you should do, and my industry to order, and get a meeting between Monsieur Discretion and you, and to make the match betwixt you.

MADAMOSEL VOLANTE
You understand me right.

DOCTOR FREEDOM
Well, I will study the means, and trye if I can procure thee a man.

MADAMOSEL VOLANTE
Good fortune be your guide.

DOCTOR FREEDOM
And Monsieur Discretion, your Husband,

[Exit.

SCENE IV

Enter **MADAMOSEL CAPRISIA**, alone.

MADAMOSEL CAPRISIA

Thoughts be at rest, for since my love is honest, and the person I love worthy, I may love honourably, for he is not only learned with study, experienced with time and practice, but he is natures favourite, she hath endued his soul with uncontrouled reason, his mind with noble thoughts, his heart with heroick generosity, and his brain with a supream wit; Besides, she hath presented his judgement and understanding, with such a clear Prospective-glasse of speculations, and such a Multiplying-glass of conception, as he seeth farther, and discerns more into natures works, than any man she hath made before him.

[She stops a little time, then speaks.

But let me consider? I have us'd this worthy Gentleman uncivilly, nay rudely, I have dispised him; wherefore he cannot love me, for nature abhors neglect, and if he cannot love me in honesty, he ought not to marry me, and if I be not his wife, for certain I shall dye for love, or live a most unhappy life, which is far worse than death. Hay ho!

[Enter **MADAM LA MERE** her Mother.

MADAM LA MERE
What, Daughter, sick with love?

MADAMOSEL CAPRISIA
O, Mother? love is a Tyrant, which never lets the mind be at rest, and the thoughts are the torments, and when the mind is tormented, the body is seldom in health.

MADAM LA MERE
Well, to ease you, I will go to this Lord Generosity, and pray him to give you a visit.

MADAMOSEL CAPRISIA
By no means, Mother, for I had rather dye with love, than live to be despised with scorn, for he will refuse your desires, or if he should come, it would be but to express his hate, or proudly triumph on my unhappy state.

[**MADAMOSEL CAPRISIA** goes out.

[**MADAM LA MERE** sola.

MADAM LA MERE
She is most desperately in love, but I will endeavour to settle her mind.

[[Exit.

SCENE V

Enter **DOCTOR FREEDOM**, and **MADAMOSEL VOLANTE**.

DOCTOR FREEDOM

Am not I a good Doctor now, that hath got you a good Husband?

MADAMOSEL VOLANTE
Nay, Doctor, he is but a Suiter, as yet.

DOCTOR FREEDOM
Why do not you woe upon the Stage, as the rest of your Comorades doth?

MADAMOSEL VOLANTE
O fye, Doctor Discretion never whines our love in publick.

DOCTOR FREEDOM
So you love to be in private?

MADAMOSEL VOLANTE
Why, Doctor, the purest love is most conceal'd, it lyes in the heart; and it warms it self by its own fire.

DOCTOR FREEDOM
Take heed, for if you keep it too tenderly, and close, it may chance to catch cold when it comes abroad.

MADAMOSEL VOLANTE
True love ought to keep home, and not to gossip abroad.

[Enter a **SERVANT-MAID**

SERVANT-MAID
Madam Monsieur Discretion is come to visit you.

MADAMOSEL VOLANTE
Come, Doctor, be a witnesse of our contract?

DOCTOR FREEDOM
I had rather stay with your Maid.

MADAMOSEL VOLANTE
She hath not wit to entertain you.

DOCTOR FREEDOM
Nor none to anger me.

MADAMOSEL VOLANTE
Pray come away, for no wise man is angry with wit.

DOCTOR FREEDOM
I perceive, if I do not go with you, that you will call me fool.

[Exit.

SCENE VI

Enter **MONSIEUR COMORADE**, and **MONSIEUR BON CAMPAIGNON**.

MONSIEUR BON CAMPAIGNON
Comorade, what cause makes you so fine to day?

MONSIEUR COMORADE
I am going to two weddings to day.

MONSIEUR BON CAMPAIGNON
Faith, one had been enough; but how can you divide yourself betwixt two Bridals?

MONSIEUR COMORADE
I shall not need to divide my self, since the Bridals keeps together; for they are marryed both in one Church, and by one Priest, and they feast in one house.

MONSIEUR BON CAMPAIGNON
And will they lye in one bed?

MONSIEUR COMORADE
No surely, they will have two beds, for fear each Bride-groom should mistake his Bride.

MONSIEUR BON CAMPAIGNON
Well, I wish the Bride-grooms, and their Brides joy, and their Guests, good chear.

MONSIEUR COMORADE
Will not you be one of the Guests?

MONSIEUR BON CAMPAIGNON
No, for a Bon Compaignon shuns Hymens Court, neither will Hymen entertain him: But who are the Brides and Bride-grooms?

MONSIEUR COMORADE
Monsieur Nobilissimo, and Madamosel Doltche, and Monsieur Perfection; and Madamosel Solid.

MONSIEUR BON CAMPAIGNON
Is Monsieur Profession a Guest there.

MONSIEUR COMORADE
No, for he swears now, that he hates marriage, as he hates death.

MONSIEUR BON CAMPAIGNON
But he loves a Mistress, as he loves life.

[Exit.

SCENE VII

Enter **MONSIEUR GENEROSITY**, and **MADAMOSEL CAPRISIA**; he following her.

MONSIEUR GENEROSITY
Lady, why do you shun my company, in going from me, praystay, and give my visit a civil entertainment; for though I am not worthy of your affection, yet my love deserves you civility.

MADAMOSEL CAPRISIA
I know you are come to laugh at me, which is ignobly done; for heroick, generous spirits, doth not triumph on the weak effeminate Sex.

MONSIEUR GENEROSITY
Pray believe I am a Gentleman, for if I loved you not, yet I would never be rude, to be uncivil to you, or your Sex; But I love you so well, as when I leave to serve you with my life, may nature leave to nourish me, fortune leave to favour me, and Heaven leave to blesse me, and then let death cast me into Hell, there to be tormented.

MADAMOSEL CAPRISIA
I am more obliged to your generous affections, than to my own merits.

MONSIEUR GENEROSITY
The ill opinion of your self doth not lessen your vertues, and if you think me worthy to be your Husband, and will agree, we will go strait to Church, and be marryed.

MADAMOSEL CAPRISIA
I shall not refuse you.

[Exit.

Margaret Cavendish – A Concise Bibliography

Philosophical Fancies (1653)
Poems and Fancies (1653)
Philosophical and Physical Opinions (1655)
Nature's Pictures drawn by Fancie's Pencil to the Life (1656)
The World's Olio (1655)
Playes, (1662) folio, containing twenty-one plays including
Loves Adventures
The Several Wits
Youths Glory, and Deaths Banquet
The Lady Contemplation
Wits Cabal

The Unnatural Tragedy
The Public Wooing
The Matrimonial Trouble
Nature's Three Daughters, Beauty, Love and Wit
The Religious
The Comical Hash
Bell in Campo
A Comedy of the Apocryphal Ladies
The Female Academy
Plays never before printed (1668), containing five plays.
The Sociable Companions, or the Female Wits
The Presence
The Bridals
The Convent of Pleasure
A Piece of a Play
Orations of Divers Sorts (1662)
Philosophical Letters, or Modest Reflections upon some Opinions in Natural Philosophy maintained by
several learned authors of the age (1664)
CCXI Sociable Letters (1664)
Observations upon Experimental Philosophy & Description of a New World (1666)
The Blazing World (1666)
The Life of William Cavendish, Duke, Marquis, and Earl of Newcastle, Earl of Ogle, Viscount Mansfield,
and Baron of Bolsover, of Ogle, Bothal, and Hepple, &c. (1667)
Grounds of Natural Philosophy (1668)

www.ingramcontent.com/pod-product-compliance
Lightning Source LLC
Chambersburg PA
CBHW021943040426
42448CB00008B/1217